Your Ride Plan for Marriage

Rick Saunders

Copyright 2009 Richard E. Saunders, All rights reserved
Published by Lulu.com Publishing, Morrisville, NC
ISBN 978-0-557-08650-4

Scripture references used in *Your Ride Plan for Marriage* are from *The Life Application Study Bible,* New Living Translation (Published by Tyndale House Publishing, Wheaton, Illinois), used by permission.

All Prepare-Enrich Material used in *Your Ride Plan for Marriage* are from the *Prepare-Enrich Couples Workbook* © 2008 (Life Innovations, Inc, Minneapolis, MN), used by permission.

All PREP material used in *Your Ride Plan for Marriage* are from the *PREP Leader Manuel* Version 7.0 © 2008 (PREP Educational Products, Inc. Greenwood Village, Co.), used by permission

Table of Contents

Introduction   vii

1. Marriage   1

2. Love   5

3. Expectations & Disappointments   7

4. Three Stages of Marriage   9

5. Roles and Responsibilities   13

6. Communication   15

7. Conflict Resolution   19

8. Finances   25

9. Sex in Marriage   29

10. Family   33

11. Children   37

Introduction

Your Ride Plan for Marriage is not intended to be a substitute for pre-marital counseling. It is designed to be a companion guide or a resource to be used by a couple to enhance or recollect on the things learned during pre-marital counseling, whether that be ongoing or years past.

This book contains a brief summarization of the pre-marital counseling that I use in my practice for preparing couples for marriage. It includes Prepare-Enrich and PREP material as well as my own, and is designed to provide you with a quick and easy resource of information that may come in useful in your marriage. Much of it you may already know; but some of it may be lost in the recesses of your mind. It is my hope that this book will help you to remember those things, and perhaps to see them in a way that you may not have while going through your pre-marital counseling.

There are many other good books and devotionals on the market that will help to enrich your marriage (some of which are listed throughout this book), and I encourage you to seek out and use as many of them as you can.

You can never learn too much about marriage.

1
Marriage

Marriage is the only game in town where both parties win or lose. From its inception in Genesis 2:24 Marriage has been designed to make a man and woman equal partners in a lifelong relationship of oneness. That is the true goal of marriage.

In the second chapter of Genesis we find Adam alone in the Garden of Eden. God has provided Adam with everything that he needs to live, yet in chapter 18 God says "It is not good for man to be alone." So what does He do? He creates a "Helpmate": A companion for Adam. The Bible tells us that he put Adam to sleep and removed one of his ribs and used that to make Eve. This was the completion of God's creation work. Unlike Adam; who was made from the dust of the ground, Eve was made from Adam's flesh and bone. In this he was demonstrating to us that marriage is the symbolic act of uniting a man and a woman as one: A mystical union uniting the hearts and lives of a couple.

In Genesis 2:24 we read: *...A man leaves his father and mother and is joined to his wife, and the two are united into one.*

The King James Version uses the word "cleave" to describe this uniting. The word used in the original text is Kollao: It means to join fast; or to glue. One way to look at this is to remember how epoxy works. Epoxy is two chemicals that when united becomes a super glue. When used correctly the two items glued together will never break where they are bonded. God is saying that this is what is happening two the man and woman when they get married. Another example of this meaning would be to take two clumps of clay and mash them together into one ball. Once done, you will never be able to separate them without leaving remnants of the two original clumps mixed together. When a man and a woman are married, even when they are apart they are still united together in a mystical oneness.

This does not mean that the couple loses their individuality; far from it. God has created everyone in a unique way. He uses that uniqueness to strengthen a marriage.

In the 1996 movie *Jerry Maguire,* the lead character played by Tom Cruise told his love interest, played by Renee Zellweger "You complete me." It was a beautiful moment and a romantic line that has been echoes in weddings ever since. Unfortunately it is not entirely accurate.

God created us as perfect human beings. The only completion necessary comes from our relationship with Jesus Christ. If we were to live our lives never getting married we are already complete. God does not put a man and a woman together to "complete them." He has created them perfect for each other. What they will then do is improve each other, bringing their unique gifts and talents into the relationship that will help to enhance those unique qualities of each other.

Marriage is a special covenant that not only unites a man and a woman into a unique oneness relationship, but it is also designed to provide that couple with a unique way to honor God and have a special relationship with him.

In my pre-marital counseling I like to use the example of a braid to illustrate the relationship between husband, wife, and God. As most of you already know; braided rope is stronger than single strand rope. In that same way, when a husband and wife both intertwine their relationship around each other, and each of them also intertwine their relationship around God, the three (Husband, wife and God) all become so linked together that they form a stronger bond than either the husband and/or wife could have alone. This is a very important aspect of God's role in your marriage. Without God, you are leaving your relationship weakened and more at risk. Keep God in your life; both individually and as a couple, and your marriage will be stronger.

That is not to say that there will not be problems. Another example I like to use concerning the braid is during the process of braiding hair. When braiding hair every so often you need to pull the hair and tighten the braid. Sometimes this process might hurt. Still, that is the process that makes the braid stronger and holds it together longer.

There are times in every relationship where things are going to hurt. It is those times that the couple who is bound together with God and each other will find that those events will make their relationship stronger.

The goal of marriage is not friendship or togetherness; it is oneness. A oneness that will unite husband and wife together in an intimate a glorious relationship that will not only satisfy and fulfill them, it will honor and glorify God.

2
Love

Before discussing love I would like to review four examples of God's description of love found in the New Testament:

For you have been called to live in freedom—not freedom to satisfy your sinful nature, but freedom to serve one another in love.

Galatians 5:13

Share each other's troubles and problems, and in this way obey the law of Christ.

Galatians 6:2

Be humble and gentle. Be patient with each other, making allowances for each other's faults because of your love.

Ephesians 4:2

Live a life filled with love for others, following the example of Christ, who loved you and gave himself as a sacrifice to take away your sins...

Ephesians 5:2

In these four verses we find some key words and phrases: "Serve one another in love"; "share each other's troubles and problems"; "humble"; "gentle"; "be patient with each other"; "make allowances for each other's faults"; "sacrifice".

Are you seeing the image here? Love is more than having a warm fuzzy for each other. It involves serving each other, being able to share burdens, accepting each other despite our faults and mistakes, humbling yourself and making sacrifices for each other. These are crucial in a loving relationship. It is these elements of love that strengthen the bonds of marriage and makes the good times into marvelous times. Love is an action verb. It goes way beyond feelings and becomes a way of life.

It is unfortunate that in the English language the word "love" has so many meanings. "I love my wife." "I love pizza." "I love riding motorcycles." Three different statements each using the word "love" but each having a very different meaning.

There are three Greek words for love that demonstrate different meanings for love:

1. Phila: Meaning brotherly love, or friendship. This is the kind of love displayed between best friends.

2. Agape: Unconditional love. The type of love provided to us by Jesus. The love we display to those we care for most of all: even when they make mistakes.

3. Eros: Sexual, erotic love.

In marriage all three of these must be present. You and your partner must be best friends. You must also have that unconditional love and respect for each other. These two components are fulfilled by following the examples in the four verses listed on the previous page.

You will obviously have sexual love, which is intended only for a husband and wife. The good news here is that if you have both Phila and Agape love: Eros will be both stronger and better!

In order to share love better you should learn to identify the ways that each of you send and receive love. A good resource for this is to purchase *The Five Love Languages* by Gary Chapman (Northfield Publishing). This will help to identify the ways that each of you communicate love and will enable you to improve your ability to communicate intimately.

3
Expectations & Disappointments

Our expectations of marriage come from many sources: Our parent's marriages provide most of those (both positive and negative). Society and the media create a lot of expectations. Our values and beliefs are another source. Expectations can come from many different areas.

There are three basic expectations that couples have when getting married:

1. The marriage will succeed: This is an obvious expectation. Couples entering a marriage obviously would not be doing so if they believed that it would end in a divorce.

2. Fidelity: This is more than just sexual fidelity. Couples are expecting faithfulness not just in the bedroom, but in all areas of their relationship: Finances, communication, not going behind each other's backs to talk negatively (or provide inappropriate intimate details) to others.

3. No problems: You would be surprised at the number of couples that I have met who believe that they will never have any serious issues or arguments. This is an unreasonable expectation and must be disposed of immediately. While the first two expectations are very reasonable, this one will lead to disillusionment and could make couples believe that their marriage was a mistake when the realities of life arrive.

After looking at the initial expectations it is time to examine personal expectations. What do you expect from marriage? What do you expect from your partner?

These expectations may be as simple as who does what around the household to things such as who is in charge of various important responsibilities. There may be sexual expectations; role expectations. The list can go on and on depending on the couple.

Expectations can make or break a marriage.

You and your partner both have them; now you must identify them. You need to first determine if your expectations are reasonable and achievable. They need to be positive and appreciate your differences as individuals and respect and cherish each other.

Once you have identified your expectations then you need to learn how to accurately communicate those expectations to your partner. Not doing so accurately will lead to disappointment.

Unmet expectations are the leading cause of disappointment. Often these unmet expectations happen because the expectation was not known. One partner may become upset with the other because something that he or she expected to be done was not done. Many times the offending partner was not even aware that the expectation was there.

[1]Expectations about love and marriage have a powerful impact on relationships. To a large degree you will be disappointed or happy in life based on how well what is happening matches up with what you think should be happening. All married couples start out hoping for and believing they will experience the very best. Problems arise when these hopes and beliefs are not based on reality

Share your expectations and make sure that they are understood; make certain that they are both realistic and achievable, and allow your partner to provide feedback. Doing so will enhance the ability to fulfill those expectations and reduce the amount of unnecessary disappointment.

Expectations and disappointments are a part of life; how we deal with them is our choice.

---

[1] Reprinted by permission. Prepare-Enrich Couples Workbook, copyright 2008, Life Innovations, Inc, Minneapolis, MN. All rights reserved.

4
Three Stages of Marriage

Marriages will ultimate go through three stages:
1. Enchantment
2. Disenchantment
3. Maturity

The Enchantment Stage is more commonly called "The Honeymoon period." This is that period of time where everything is wonderful. The couple is so blinded by their love for each other that even the bad is good. Sometimes this is the stage where those around the couple may want to get sick after witnessing the excessive lovey-dovey behavior for too long. Still, this is a wonderful time in a marriage. While the initial rapture fades, the enchantment stage will usually last for quite a while. On average it will continue for seven years. For some couples it will end much sooner and others it will last longer. The time that it last does not necessarily have anything to do with the strength or weakness of your marriage; but rather the individual personalities of each partner and what is going on around them. So do not be concerned if your enchantment stage does not last as long as others.

The Disenchantment Stage is probably the most important stage of a marriage that most couples never learn about. If you have ever bought a new car you probably remember how well you treated it at first. You were careful how you parked it. You never left trash in it. You kept it clean and babied it. Then, eventually, it just became 'the car'. Whether you want to believe it or not, the same thing will happen with your marriage. Maybe not to the extreme of 'the car', but it will happen.

In every marriage there comes a time when one partner begins to feel less enthused about the relationship than they used to be. It will happen to both partners, just not always at the same time.

As already mentioned, this occurs once the Enchantment Stage ends: on average around the seventh year of the marriage. Do you recall the phrase: 'The seven year itch'? That is a prime example of a negative response to this stage.

Many marriages end in uncontested divorces because "We just fell out of love." Love is a choice and not something that you simply fall into or out of. Many of these marriages end because one or both partners are in this stage and honestly believe that they fell out of love or that the marriage just is not worth saving. At times these feelings become excuses for adultery.

Couples need to understand that this stage will occur at some point in your marriage. If you know that and anticipate it then you can work through it more easily. I have had couples come to me who realized that this was happening and instead of giving up they worked through it and have stronger marriages now than before.

The first thing that you need to do when you recognize this stage is to inform your partner: Easier said than done. That will no doubt bring up one of those disappointments we discussed in the previous chapter. Find a way to share it in as loving a way as possible, but do it. Then agree to work together to get through it. It does not have to be a long tedious process. There are many ways to do it. Sometimes the couple can work through this on their own. Or you may attend a marriage enhancement seminar. You can attend marriage counseling. The important thing to remember is to not give up.

My best recommendation for couples is to prepare for this from the beginning. Never stop dating. Keep the romance in your relationship. This is especially important for us men who sometimes feel that once we have won our wife we no longer have to pursue her. Big mistake!

Keep the romance in your marriage; build good communication skills and you will find it much easier and quicker to cross this speed bump.

The Maturity stage is that phase that begins once you have moved through the Disenchantment stage. This has nothing to do with being old, but rather maturing and developing a loving relationship that you will carry with you as you grow old.

This is when you almost fall in love all over again. It is better than the initial stage because now you value your relationship even more than before. There will still be problems, you might even find the Disenchantment Stage trying to rear up again, but overall the marriage is at a point where it is maturing and growing into something that the couple may never have believed possible.

5
Roles and Responsibilities

What is your role in your marriage? Who does what and who is responsible for what? Failure to clarify roles can cause a major disruption. There are many experts who will provide you with many different answers and suggestions to these questions. God has equipped men and women for different tasks, but all tasks lead to the same goal: honoring God. That is the ultimate responsibility for our roles; and it does not matter what sex we are. There is no reason to ever think that either sex is superior to the other.

Even so, you will find it necessary to identify roles in the relationship. Many times when roles come up people become concerned or even outright upset over the prospect of "wives submitting to their husbands" coming up. Please allow me to explain that in a way that might make sense:

The word "submit" has taken on a negative meaning; but that is not necessarily how Paul intended it to be. In Gal, 3:28 Paul emphasized the equality of all believers in Christ. So when he brings up submitting in Ephesians 5 he is talking about believers submitting by choice. For the wife Paul is implying that she should honor her husband; making him second only to Jesus Christ; not that she is to be his submissive servant.

If you read the rest of Ephesians 5 you will find several verses of instruction telling the husband how he is to love and honor his wife in order to earn that place of honor.

Now that we have moved beyond that, let's take a practical look at roles and responsibilities: The checkbook must be balanced, the bills must be paid, the laundry must be done, and meals must be prepared... the list goes on and on.

Someone has to do this. Is it the role of the husband or the wife? Yes!

The couple needs to examine their gifts, the abilities; their time and resources and make a decision as to who does what. None of these are male/female issues. They are practical decisions that must be made by determining who can do what the best. Often the couple will share many of these tasks equally; other times this will not be the case.

Each marriage is different. Often your experiences growing up may cause you to assume certain roles. Sometimes that works, sometimes it won't. Do not assume anything; discuss it and come to a positive decision as to how things will get done in your marriage. And do not worry if your neighbors do it the same way. Once more, this is where God's unique design for each of you will come into play as you share responsibilities equally and recognize each partner's gifts and talents and allow them to use them accordingly.

6
Communication

What happens to the body without blood?

You die.

Communication is to a relationship what blood is to the body. It is a necessary component to keep the relationship not only alive; but thriving. It is very important to learn how to communicate well.

There are three components in every message:

1. The Content of the message
2. Tone of Voice
3. Non-Verbal Communication.

Of the three, the actual content is the smallest component of of a message. According to studies, the content makes up as little as 7% of the message. We tend to rely more on non-verbal communication (Body Language) and tone of voice more than anything else. Think about it: Have you ever noticed how so many people misunderstand text messages and e-mail messages, believing that someone was upset or not understanding the content correctly. It was written down for them to read, but they still misunderstood it. That is because we are so conditioned to rely on body language and tone of voice that we sometimes have difficulty when all we have is the content to depend on.

Of the three, body language is the biggest component of a message. It can make up as much as 55% of the message: That's more than half! Your stance, the way you move your eyes, pounding your fist; these and so many other actions say more than your words when you communicate.

Tone of voice can make up as much as 38% of your message. I'm sure everyone reading this has asked the question "How are you?" And received a cold, monotone *"Fine,"* answer that let us know immediately that all was not well.

The fact is that the statement, "It's not what you say, it's how you say it." is truer than you ever knew.

Communication is the process of sharing yourself, verbally and non-verbally, in such a way that your partner can both accept and understand what you are sharing.

The biggest hindrance to communication is the illusion that it has already happened. That is why you must become proficient in communication.

Prepare-Enrich, one of the leaders in building stronger marriages, explains two primary components to communication that I have included on the following pages of this chapter:

[2] 2 Primary Components to Communication: <u>Assertiveness</u> and <u>Active Listening</u>

Assertiveness: The ability to express your feelings and ask for what you want in the relationship.

Assertiveness is a valuable communication skill. In successful couples, both individuals tend to be quite assertive. Rather than assuming their partner can read their minds, they share how they feel and ask clearly and directly for what they want.

- Use "I" statements.
- Avoid statements beginning with "you".
- Make constructive requests that are positive and respectful.
- Use polite phrases such as "please" and "thank you".

Example: "I want to go skiing on vacation, but I know that you like going to the beach. I would like to discuss our options to help decide what we should do."

---

[2] Reprinted by permission. Prepare-Enrich Couples Workbook, copyright 2008, Life Innovations, Inc, Minneapolis, MN. All rights reserved

Active Listening:

Active Listening is the ability to let your partner know you understand them by restating their message.

- Good Communication depends on you carefully listening to another person.
- Active Listening involves listening attentively without interruption.
- It includes restating what was heard;
- Acknowledging the content and feelings of the speaker.

The Active Listening process lets the speaker know whether or not the message they sent was clearly understood.

- When each person knows what the other person feels and wants (assertiveness) and when each knows they have been heard and understood (active listening), intimacy is increased.
- These two communication skills can help you grow closer as a couple.

- **Communication Skills to increase intimacy**
  1. **Give full attention to your partner when talking.** Turn off the phone, shut off the TV, make eye contact.
  2. **Focus on the good qualities in each other and often praise each other.** A good way to be assertive without being critical is to use "I" rather than "you" statements.
  3. **Be assertive.** Share your thoughts, feelings, and needs.
  4. **Avoid criticism.**
  5. **If you must criticize, balance it with at least one positive comment.** (i.e. "I appreciate how you take the trash out each week. In the future can you remember to bring the trash can back from the street?")
  6. **Listen to understand, not to judge.**
  7. **Use Active Listening.** Summarize your partner's comments before sharing your own reactions or feelings.
  8. **Avoid blaming each other and work together for a solution.**
  9. Use the ten step approach (We will talk more about that later).
  10. **Seek counseling if you are unable to resolve an issue, before it becomes more serious.**

Here are some simple ideas that will help to build better communication:
- Daily Dialogue and Daily Compliments:
- Set aside time to just talk to each other about each other and the things you enjoy in addition to the usual discussion of the daily activities.
- Give your partner at least one genuine compliment each day (general or specific)
- Spend time together each day in prayer and Bible reading or devotional time.

7
Conflict Resolution

Conflict is a fact of life. No matter how much you love each other and how well you communicate there will be times when conflict is inevitable. The important thing is not that it occurs, but how you deal with it. [3]Studies show the amount of disagreements is not related to marital happiness as much as how they are handled. Happy couples do not avoid disagreements; they resolve them while remaining respectful of each other, Thereby strengthening their relationship.

The use of 'weapons' in conflict must be avoided. By weapons I do not mean physical violence: we all know that **there is no place for physical or emotional abuse or violence in a relationship** (or elsewhere for that matter), so we are going on the assumption that this is accepted. If you suffer any abuse then you need to notify the authorities and get away from the situation as quickly as possible!

By weapons I am referring to other things that can be used by one partner against the other during conflict; such as insults, raised voices, bringing up the past, using sex (or denial of sex) as a tool, and many more things.

It is also not wise to use words like "never" or "always" as these definitive statements will cancel out your point. For example, if you say, "You never take out the garbage." Your partner may reply "That's not true; I did it once last month. The use of such words will often backfire.

---

[3] Reprinted by permission. Prepare-Enrich Couples Workbook, copyright 2008, Life Innovations, Inc, Minneapolis, MN. All rights reserved

When you are dealing with conflict you have the option of one of the following: Yield, withdraw, compromise, win, or resolve. The worst of these is to withdraw as it is giving up (More on that later). The best possible option is to resolve the conflict. Resolving usually leads to the relationship being strengthened.

Rather than reinvent the wheel I will be providing you with information from [4]PREP and [5]Prepare-Enrich over the next few pages that will greatly help you in learning how to deal with conflict and bring about a positive resolution to your relationship.

(Author's Note: Items prefixed with (4) are PREP, (5) are Prepare-Enrich, (A) are the author's comments).

(A) In dealing with conflict you need to be able to recognize the danger signs that will make things worse. PREP offers four communication danger signs, which are:

(4)

Four Communication Danger Signs:

1. **Escalation**: When partners respond back and forth negatively with each other.
   - Makes you feel less emotionally safe.
   - Often results in hurtful words or actions.
2. **Invalidation**: When one partner puts down the thoughts, feelings, or character of the other.
   - Subtle: "Why can't you ever do anything right?"
   - Extreme: "You are a pathetic loser."
   - Using hurtful things against your partner that were shared at intimate times. This may create a boundary preventing future sharing.
3. **Negative Interpretations**: When one partner makes a negative and unfair assumption about what the other partner was thinking.
   - Hearing things more negatively than they are.

---

[4] Reprinted by permission. PREP Version 7.0 Leader Manual, Scott M. Stanley, Howard J. Markman, Natalie Jenkins, Susan Blumberg, copyright 2008, PREP Educational Products Inc. Greenwood Village, CO. All rights reserved.

[5] Reprinted by permission. Prepare-Enrich Couples Workbook, copyright 2008, Life Innovations, Inc, Minneapolis, MN. All rights reserved

- Believing the worst.
- Seeing what we "expect" to see.
- These can lead to damaging assumptions about your partner's actions that may not be true.
- They are very hard to detect and counteract after they become cemented into the fabric of a relationship.
- Kids learn this from their parents (He did it on purpose; it wasn't an accident." Everything becomes personal.
4. **Avoidance and Withdrawal**: When one partner is unwilling to stay with an important discussion.
- Can be as obvious as walking out during an argument.
- The withdrawer often tends to get quiet during an argument, or may agree quickly to some suggestion just to end the conversation, with no real intention of following through.
- Often results in negative interpretations about why the other is withdrawing; or why the other won't "back off."
- Often when one person withdraws the other pursues. (Follows; continues; gets louder).
- The one who pursues often doesn't want to fight, they want to connect. The one withdrawing is not trying to pull away from the partner, but rather the conflict.

(A) Negatives are very powerful: Some researches estimate that one negative counteracts anywhere from 5 to 20 positives in a marriage.

(4)
Effects of Danger Signs on Children:
- Feeling scared
- Feeling sad
- Blaming themselves for the conflict.
- Problems with school.
- Worrying about their parents breaking up.
- More likely to experience the danger signs in their own relationships.

Minimizing stress for children:
- Avoid escalating.
- Show each other respect while you disagree.
- Use conflict resolution skills.

- Help children feel secure by talking to them about their feelings and saying "I love you."

(4)
Ten Steps for Resolving Conflict:
1. Set a time and place for discussion
2. Define the problem – be specific.
3. List the ways you each contribute to the problem (Each list both)
4. List past attempts to resolve the issue that was not successful.
5. Brainstorm—pool your new ideas and try to list 10 possible solutions to the problem. Do not judge or criticize any of the suggestions at this point.
6. Discuss and evaluate each of these possible solutions—be as objective as possible.
7. Agree on one solution to try.
8. Agree how you will each work toward this solution (Be as specific as possible).
9. Set up another meeting to discuss your progress.
10. Reward each other for progress. (If you notice your partner making a positive contribution toward the solution, praise his/her effort.)

(5)
Taking a Time Out

Sometimes a conflict becomes too heated. Rather than permitting things to escalate into something that will have negative results, it will be wise to take a time out to cool down.

1. **Recognize your need for a time out**. (Clenched fists, red face, breathing fast, crying, shouting, etc.) Learn to recognize the signs that things have become too intense and what triggers cause you to have negative physical and/or emotional reactions.
2. **Request the time out**. Say something like "I'm just too angry to talk right now. I need to take a time out." Perhaps it is useful to have an agreed upon code word. Agree on a specific time when you will be ready to resume. (Minimum 30 minutes, maximum 24 hours). Grant your partner's request.
3. **Relax and Calm Down**. Take some deep breaths. Go for a walk, do calming exorcizes, write, pray; whatever works for you.

4. Remember what's important.
- Try to identify what you were thinking and feeling that became so difficult to discuss.
- Think about "I" messages you could use to tell your partner what you were thinking or feeling, and what you need from them.
- Try to spend some quiet time considering your partner's point of view and what they are feeling.
- Remember that the two of you are a team, and the only way your relationship will win is if you work toward a resolution that both individuals can feel good about.
- Resume the conversation. Use assertiveness and active listening skills/the 10-steps for conflict—or use the Speaker/Listener approach.

Speaker/Listener technique

(A) The Speaker/Listener technique as an excellent tool that will enable the couple to speak calmly in order to share their thoughts and feelings in a safe manner and will allow for better understanding. This is not intended to be used for normal conversations; but rather when situations arise where conflict might otherwise escalate, or to help resolve the situation when escalation has already occurred.

This method often works best if something is used to identify who the speaker is (i.e. the Native American Talking Feather approach). PREP uses a pre-printed card with instructions, but anything that the couple agrees upon may be used.

The following information is provided by PREP:

(4)
Speaker/Listener technique is:
- A way to talk safely when you really need to do it well.
- Not designed to be used all the time.
- Neutralizes the Danger Signs.
- Regular practice can help to "inoculate" your relationship against Danger Signs.
- It is for each partner to feel understood by the other.
- It is not an agreement.
- It is not to solve the problem (yet)

Rules for the Speaker:
- Speak for yourself, don't mind read!
- Keep statements brief. Don't go on and on.
- Stop to let the listener paraphrase.

Rules for the Listener:
- Paraphrase what you hear.
- Focus on the speaker's message. Don't rebut.

Rules for Both:
- The Speaker has the floor.
- Speaker keeps the floor while the listener paraphrases.
- Share the floor.
  - Paraphrasing does not come naturally, so getting comfortable with it is important.

How to paraphrase:
  - So, what I hear you saying is…
  - It sounds like you are saying…

Steps:

Speaker: Speaks.

Listener: Paraphrases, then asks, "Did I get that right."

Speaker: Yes or no. If no, say it again.

8
Finances

The Bible has a lot to say about money. Money was one of the most talked about topics by Jesus, and is still one of the most debated topics in the Bible. There are well over 2000 verses in the Bible about money, with over 800 of them speaking directly on the topic of money management. The number of verses in the Bible about money total more than the number of verses about Heaven and Hell combined.

The main reason for this is that on average we do not necessarily deal with pure Heaven and Hell issues on a daily basis; but we most probably deal with money every day of our lives. So it is only natural that God wants to provide us with information to enable us to live right, especially where money is concerned.

Your attitude toward money and your past lifestyle may be a very hard adjustment for you when you marry. Financial difficulties can place a strain on the marital relationship.

There are decisions to be made concerning your finances from day one: Who will pay the bills and balance the checkbook? Will you have one checking account or two? I cannot provide a right or wrong answer for you on these types of questions. This must be determined by each couple using their best judgment after reviewing their abilities and desires.

There are some other areas concerning finance that we can look at: the first of which is very important: Make a budget!

Many people hate the 'B' word, but I assure you that a budget is essential in keeping your finances in order. It is not difficult to do and you can find an abundance of good budgeting resources on the Internet, book stores and libraries.

Here are some common sense suggestions to use when preparing a budget:

1. Plan your budget together.
2. Define goals.
3. Don't rush into it.
4. Use common sense.
5. Don't budget for other's lifestyles.
6. Adjust your budget over a period of three months.
7. Don't quit!
8. Include God in your goal setting. He will give you the discipline you need.

In all probability your budget will be wrong when you first create it. That is to be expected, continue working on it the first few months until it is accurate. Then review it every three months or so for the first year. After that you should only have to review it annually unless there are changes to your income or bills.

Once you have your budget, USE IT! A budget in the drawer does no good. You must follow your budget if you expect your finances to stay in order.

One mistake that many young couples make is to try to keep up the lifestyle that they were used to at home. You need to remember that your parents probably did not live that same lifestyle when they first started out, so why should you expect to do so. Avoid the temptation to live above your means or to use credit to buy those luxuries that you might have been used to at home. Follow your budget and spend wisely and you should eventually work your way up to being able to afford many of those things without the need for credit.

Finances can be the cause of a lot of difficulties in marriages. That is why you need to have good communication concerning your spending with each other. You also need to know the dangers of using money either as power or for self-esteem.

If you have not already done so I would recommend that couples take a financial management class. One excellent source is

Dave Ramsey's Financial Peace University. There are many other good courses and books out there too.

Learn to identify your financial patterns and how your family dealt with money. These can create financial habits that might carry over into your marriage. For example, someone who grew up in a family that lived paycheck to paycheck is used to looking at finances from a different perspective than someone who grew up in a family that had enough income to not only stay ahead of the bills, but could afford to by luxuries at will. If children from these two families marry then one may instinctively be very cautious about spending even when the money is there, or the other may spend at will even when the money is not there. The two different viewpoints may create difficulties. So it is important to discuss your view and history of finance with your partner.

If you have any difficulties with finance, or believe that you or your partner has problems with not being able to control spending, then do not let these things continue. Seek help or counseling immediately before it is too late.

Tithing

We cannot look at the topic of finances without looking at tithing. No matter what our situation is we need to recognize that all we have is God's to begin with and that he has chosen to loan it to us (even when it does not appear to be enough). God provides for us and He wants us to be faithful and to share our blessings with others.

Tithing is very important; but do not look at it as a "name it/claim it" process. God will indeed bless our tithes and offerings, and He will bless us for giving, but this is not a money making scheme. Your attitude towards tithing is very important. If you give seeking recognition or profit then why should God bless your tithe; you have already received what you sought. And if you tithe begrudgingly then you might as well not tithe at all.

When you give, do so with a joyful heart. Our gifts are to be something that we enjoy giving as a means of helping others. Tithing is one of the ways that God provides us to help reach the world for Christ.

That brings up another question: How much do I give?

The word tithe comes from the book of Malachi when the Israelites were told to bring their tithe to the storehouse. The word tithe means one-tenth. So the common thinking is that 10% is the suggested amount. I am not telling you to give 10%. My suggestion is that—as a couple—you seek God's will through prayer and ask Him how much you should give, and then give whatever amount He instructs you to give with a loving and prayerful heart.

In chapter 3 of Malachi God says "Test me" in reference to tithing. This is one of the few times in Scripture where God says to test Him. Act in faith and give what the Lord leads you to give, and do so for the right reasons, and you will see god bless your gifts and you in mighty ways.

9
Sex in Marriage

The Bible talks about four specific purposes for human sexual activity:

- Procreation
- Recreation
- Communication
- Release

We find procreation in Genesis 1:28 when God instructs Adam and Eve to *be fruitful and multiply.* But that is not where it ends. God designed sex to be a beautiful and enjoyable act between husband and wife. Dr. Tony Evans describes sex as a fire that in the fireplace is a wonderful and beautiful thing, but in the curtains is a disaster.

Sex in marriage is to be enjoyed. It is the single most intimate form of communication that a couple can share. It was intended for a husband and wife to totally and completely reveal themselves to each other, pouring out all of their energies and affections into your spouse. It is the ultimate fulfillment of Genesis 2:24 for becoming "one flesh."

The enjoyment of sex between husband and wife can be found referenced in the Song of Solomon. Proverbs 5:18 tells us that it is meant to satisfy each other. Sex provides a means of presenting your spouse with the gift of yourself, a deeper means of saying, "I love you." In short it becomes a mode of communication, of knowing each other and is mutually enjoyable. Communication in this area is as important as communication in other areas of your marriage.

In order to for sex to be what it was intended to be in your marriage you must make certain that it remains within the boundaries of marriage. Proverbs 5:15-19 says: *Drink water from your own well— share your love only with your wife. Why spill the water from your spring in public, having sex with just anyone? You should reserve it for yourselves. Don't share it with strangers. Let your wife be a fountain of blessing for you. Rejoice in the wife of your youth. She is a loving doe, a graceful dear. Let her breasts satisfy you always. May you always be captivated by her love.*

In the dessert water is precious. In Old Testament times it was a crime to steal water from someone else's well. You must reserve your sexual love for your spouse alone, not waste it outside of marriage. Unlike what we see in society today, God wants us to seek satisfaction and companionship from our partner alone. When you follow God's design for sex you will find something more precious and enjoyable than anything else that the world has to offer.

When it comes to sex, the couple needs to be open and honest with each other. Disclose your past history in appropriate ways so that no secrets can arise to cause discomfort in the relationship. You need to be open and understanding with each other's past; it will affect your future intimacy.

When it comes to children you need to decide if and when you want children, and agree on birth control options should you wish to wait. It is also very important that you discuss concerns or fears about sex. This includes sharing intimate acts that you cannot or will not participate in with your partner, and to respect those things that have been shared with you. One important reason for this is that if your partner attempts something that you cannot or will not do, a simple "stop it" may be looked upon as a rejection of them. Telling them why will help them to understand that they are not being rejected, the act is.

For those who are not yet married, please remember that your wedding day may be very stressful; especially for the bride. By the time you reach your destination after the wedding and the reception you may be too exhausted to do anything more than sleep. If this is how you or your partner feels, do not let it be a concern. It is not a sign that you made a mistake. It is a sign that you are tired. Do not force something to be one more 'requirement' of your wedding night. If it happens, great! If you are tired, wait.

It is also very possible that your wedding night may not be able to live up to your expectations. Once again, do not worry, it will get better.

If you have ever read the book *His Needs Her Needs* then you have probably seen the top five needs for husbands and wives. According to the book, the number 1 need for husbands is sex, while the number 1 need for wives is affection.

Do you see how this could cause a conflict?

Let's look at the husband first: Technically the book is both right and wrong about the number 1 need of husbands being sex. Actually, the number 1 need for husbands is respect. Most men relate respect coming from their wives with sex.

Men are visual and logical creatures and tend to desire sex in a more visual and direct way. While women are more emotion driven and can receive pleasure without necessarily having sex. While this appears to put husbands and wives on a collision course, that is only true if everything only goes one way.

Husbands, keep the romance alive. Show your wives how much you love her. Take your time, touch and caress her and fulfill her needs for affection.

Wives; respond in kind, enjoy the affection and sometimes just go for it.

Together you will find that the variety and romance will lead to a fulfilling and satisfactory sexual relationship.

While on the subject of sex; please remember that this is one very important area where fidelity is important in other ways than being sexually faithful to each other. You need to also know how to keep your mouths shut.

In the book *The Samson Syndrome* the author suggests that there should be 10 intimate details that only you know about your spouse. If you cannot come up with ten things off the top of your head then perhaps you are sharing too much with the wrong people.

10
Family

The Book of Ruth provides us with a phenomenal picture of what an in-law relationship should be. After her husband dies, (along with Naomi's husband and other son), Ruth disregards her mother-in-laws suggestion that she go find another husband and returns to Israel with Naomi in order to help care for her mother-in-law.

In today's society parents and in-laws are looked upon as meddlesome and ignorant at best. Television sit-coms almost always portray extended family as dysfunctional and inept.

In all likelihood when you get married you will be getting a new set of family members to go along with the ones that you already have. And that can bring about a whole new realm of challenges. Fortunately, if handled correctly it can bring a new realm of blessings too.

Often—especially during the wedding process—parents can interfere and be a little overbearing even when they have the best of intentions. This is usually the result of one of two things: Try as we might; we parents still see our children as children. It is just so hard for us to recognize that they are really grown up adults. That's the good one. The second is that sometimes parents just see a need to continue trying to run your life. If that is the case then you will need to establish boundaries early on.

You are your spouse are a new family unit. I performed a wedding in Florida where after the ceremony I heard someone say to the bride and groom, "From this moment on you are family; everyone else are just relatives."

That statement is very true. The new husband and wife are to be the core of this new relationship in order to grow as a couple, but you must also maintain a positive relationship with both sides of the family.

If your parents are acting a little different as your wedding nears try to remember that they are going through a grieving process. This is especially true if you are young and this is your first marriage. While your parents are happy for you, they are experience a loss on several levels and may not know how to deal with it, if they even recognize it. Give them the benefit of the doubt and things should improve soon after the wedding. If not, then you may have other issues.

You and your spouse need to decide what is and is not interference by extended family members. Be reasonable; not everything is interference. Interference is when family members try to impose their will on you without concern of your desires or opinions. Often they disguise this as "suggestions." Keep in mind that a suggestion gives you the right to say no. If no is not an option then it is not a suggestion, it is a demand.

You need to work together to establish boundaries when interference does occur. Utilize the techniques you learned for communication to help in this area.

As a couple, you also need to be aware of any emotional ties that one or both of you might have with your parents that could cause difficulties in your relationship. You need to continue contact, but there should not be any apron strings preventing the husband and wife from bonding as the primary focus of this new marriage.

Review your family upbringing. Think of things from your parent's marriage that you want to have in your marriage. At the same time, try to identify things in their marriage that you do not want to have in your marriage.

We are creatures of habit, and we tend to duplicate what we learn. Those things are parents did that we like will be easy to do. So will those things that we do not like. Identify any such problem areas up front and work together with your partner to find a way to prevent those from being repeated in your marriage now before they take a foothold and start to grow.

Decide early on where you plan to spend your first Thanksgiving and Christmas. Do not assume that your families know what your plans are. If you do not tell them then they are probably expecting you to be with them. This could create hurt feelings if not handled correctly. Share your plans and tell your family why and they will usually understand.

What do you plan to call your partner's parents? Mom and Dad; Mr. and Mrs. _____; Hey you.

You have to call them something. My suggestion is for each partner to go to their parents and say, "Mom, Dad, what do you want to be called?"

They will find it easier to answer truthfully to you than to their child's new spouse.

Families can and will present challenges. The good news is that when you handle this correctly you will often find yourself surrounded by a new loving family. There is no guarantee, but the least you can do is your part.

11
Children

Are you planning on having children?

If you already have children please move on to the next section. For those of you who do not have children yet here is some helpful advice:

If you already know that you want children, and how many, share that information with your partner. You need to make sure that you are on the same page. You should also discuss what you would do if you have an unexpected pregnancy before you planned to have a child. Or what you would do if you learn that you cannot have children.

If you plan to wait before having children then discuss how you plan not to have them. Ignoring this will usually mean children arriving before you had anticipated it.

Discuss your plans for childcare. Will one of you stay home with the child while the other works? Will you use daycare? Do you anticipate having family watch them? You better check with the family before deciding on that option to make sure that they agree.

Determine what—if anything—you would do different raising children than what your parents did.

Discuss discipline methods with your partner. The same is true for church and values. Both partners need to be in agreement on these issues.

Blended Families

Blended/stepfamilies bring different challenges. These families can be just as loving and caring for each other as traditional families, but they will take a little more effort to build strong relationships. The good news is that the effort is worth it.

You must first do away with some of the step-family myths that often result in disappointment.

Just because you and your spouse are in love you cannot assume that the stepchildren will have those same feelings. It will take time for bonding between stepsiblings and stepparents. Remember that in most cases the children had no say in this marriage. Give them time to adjust. And there are times when some children will never bond with their new families.

Stepparents often make the mistake of trying too hard to bond with their new stepchildren. This can cause the child to push away. It is very important to allow the child to set the pace for the development of this new relationship.

The first two years of creating a stepfamily can be as stressful as the first two years following a divorce. Give the children time. Usually younger children will adjust more quickly than older children. Do not be disappointed that the children to not respond right away. There are even times when a child will try to sabotage the relationship in hopes that his or her biological parents will get back together. Staying united and continuing to love the children will in most cases eventually win out.

Whatever the situation, the couple must give priority to the marriage and each other, not just the children.

Love is patient and kind. Love is not jealous or boastful or proud or rude. Love does not demand its own way. Love is not irritable, and it keeps no record of when it has been wronged. It is never glad about injustice but rejoices whenever the truth wins out. Love never gives up, never loses faith, is always hopeful, and endures through every circumstance. Love never fails...

I Corinthians 13: 4-8

28 Days: Riding with the King

By Rick Saunders

A four-week biker devotional designed to help kick start the riding season the right way: spending time with the King before hitting the road.

This devotional is not just for bikers. It is for anyone who has the heart of a biker and a quest for adventure; anyone who wants to have live, and that more abundantly, by allowing Jesus to be your Road Captain, taking you on a journey that will inspire and motivate you to have all the Christ promised you as a child of the King.

Published by lulu.com publishing

Available at:
www.28DaysRidingWithTheKing.com
Amazon.com
BarnesandNobel.com
Lule.com
And other on-line book sellers

All proceeds go to the Christian Motorcyclists Association's
Run for the Son missions outreach

Made in the USA
Middletown, DE
03 February 2023

23843532R00031